Luna BELLA Luna

A PORTRAIT OF VESALE, ITALY

Published by Mohawk Paper Mills, Inc.
P.O. Box 497, 465 Saratoga Street, Cohoes, New York 12047

Produced by VSA Partners, Inc.
542 South Dearborn, Suite 202, Chicago, Illinois 60605
Designed by James Koval
Assisted by Steven Ryan

Written by Michael Noble
Edited and translated by Alba Rosso Dwass

Photographs by Paul Elledge
1808 West Grand Avenue, Chicago, Illinois 60622

PRINTED IN THE UNITED STATES BY THE STINEHOUR PRESS, LUNENBURG, VERMONT
ON MOHAWK SUPERFINE WHITE, SOFTWHITE, AND ULTRAWHITE.

ISBN 0-9657333-0-0 (hardback)
ISBN 0-9657333-1-9 (softback)

Luna BELLA *Luna*

A PORTRAIT OF VESALE, ITALY

Photographs by Paul Elledge

Luna, bella luna speaks to the importance of simplicity, integrity, and character. Our aim was to capture and honestly portray the essence of things well made and the nature of lives well lived. We at Mohawk Paper Mills hope it reminds you, as it does us, of the more timeless virtues and traditions that endure in a swiftly changing world. One reason Mohawk Superfine was selected for the project is its connection to these same lasting elements of quality and craftsmanship. See for yourself how these finely printed images are so easily integrated into the sheet's very fabric. Notice how one thing compliments and enhances the other so seamlessly. This, too, reminds us of Davide and Ermelina and how the ways of life are supposed to work.

MOHAWK PAPER MILLS, INC.

This book is warmly dedicated to my parents, Frances and James Elledge, who always encouraged me to follow my heart and honor the truth. I also must express sincere gratitude to Davide and Ermelina Querciagrossa, as well as their wonderful and extended family, for the honor and privilege of sharing their lives with me.

Dedico questo libro ai miei genitori, Frances e James Elledge, che mi hanno sempre incoraggiato a onorare la verità e ad andare dove mi porta il cuore. Desidero inoltre esprimere la mia più sincera gratitudine a Davide ed Ermelina Querciagrossa e a tutta la loro meravigliosa famiglia, per avermi concesso l'onore e il privilegio di fare un po' di strada insieme a loro.

PAUL ELLEDGE

Walking up the hill, as he's done every day, at least twice a day, since he was a boy, Davide Querciagrossa laughingly recites the words... Luna, bella luna fammi sognar dormendo chi sposerò vivendo. Moon, beautiful moon, make me dream while I am sleeping about whom I will marry when I awake. These lines have been etched on Davide's heart since adolescence, and he can no longer remember when or why he and his friends arranged them this way. Like other things Davide is fond of saying, this little poem serves as a prayer or a joke depending on his mood, which by the way, is difficult to know since Davide's feelings rarely come to the surface.

He's nothing like his wife, Ermelina, whom he married while very much awake more than fifty years ago. She is open and frank, as uncomplicated and neat as her kitchen. Ask Ermelina a question, almost any question, and you'll receive an honest answer, usually followed by a story. Ermelina loves to talk, especially about her family.

The two of them have lived in the same house since they were married. Together they raised two sons here, Adriano and Giuliano. Adriano and his wife Rosa live upstairs with their son Gianluca. Giuliano is married, too. He and his wife Renata used to live in the family's other house, which is located just a short walk from Davide and Ermelina's. Now they have a place in Modena, but their newly married daughter, Sabrina, lives in the house with her husband. On weekends, they often return for church and dinner and the love of family conversation.

More than twelve years ago, Sabrina's cousin Judy, who lives in America, came to visit with her husband Paul Elledge. That's when Paul began photographing this family. Over the years, he's returned again and again to northern Italy and the tiny mountain village called Vesale to be with these people, to learn their language and customs, and to document with honor a way of life the moon has witnessed for countless generations.

Much can be said about these photographs, but most of all they demonstrate one artist's honest appreciation for history, tradition, and lives well lived. And in all these photographs one can see the caring observations of an outsider. Paul pays close attention to things Davide and Ermelina take for granted. "Why would you come all this way to photograph a fence?" asks an amused and bewildered Davide.

But Paul doesn't mind. He places all his subjects in context. The family and their neighbors are always seen in the midst of life, surrounded by the hills, the earth and the sky that inform their experience. And they are also seen closely, in detail, because that way one can grasp evidence of the more subtle virtues. Paul is considered one of the family here, and it's not difficult for him to unite himself with the people and the countryside he portrays on film.

Through his lens, he sees much in this life that is simple, heroic and genuine. But he also sees a serenity that is vanishing before his eyes.

Things are changing in Vesale, as they are changing in similar places throughout the world. Ancient customs and traditions that link us to the past are yielding to new and different demands. Most of the people in Vesale are old. Davide and Ermelina are both in their seventies. Many of the children have moved to the valley, abandoning the slow and skillful work that has been handed down from father to son and mother to daughter seemingly since the dawn of time. In place of cows and orchards, the younger people tend machines in computerized factories, and instead of the homemade meals, the young people eat fast food because now they are in a hurry.

Despite the pace and pressures of modern life, the old ways endure. Davide's grandchildren carry on. Sabrina who grew up in Modena chooses now to live in Vesale with her husband. Gianluca, who is an engineering student and could easily build his career in Milan, also plans to remain in the family's household. And Fabrizio, who studied agriculture, remains in the family's hometown and creates among other things outstanding balsamic vinegar. Together they sustain the endless rhythms of family.

Luna, bella luna sings his grandfather as he starts down the hill. Think of the moon as you view these images, that unblinking witness to all our delights and disasters, and consider the timeless, elemental aspects of human experience.

LA REGIONE

There is something eccentric and paradoxical about this land. The mountains here are relatively young, active, and bubbling with underground springs. Just beneath the surface there is ample evidence of ancient cultures. The Etruscans were here long before the Romans; and long before humans settled here, woolly mammoths prowled the area. A typical Sunday outing in spring is formed around a father showing his young daughter where the fossilized bones of such a creature were found.

Monte Cimone is the highest mountain in these parts, and in winter it is a favorite spot for skiing. In summer it is even more popular, for in summer the upper shoulders of this mountain are covered with wild berries, especially blackberries. People come from miles around to pick and savor those berries. Also in the warmer seasons, the hills and valleys near Vesale erupt in colorful and scented vegetation.

Cherry trees dominate the lower valleys and the countryside is loaded with oaks, chestnuts and brooms. Wild mushrooms thrive in these woods, and in the fields a sea of poppies undulates in the easy summer breeze. But a more subtle, and memorable emblem of summer is the aroma of hay drying in the afternoon sun. That's what Rosa, Davide's daughter-in-law, enjoys the most about summer. That, and the perfume of water and earth that lingers in the air after a thunderstorm rolls through the valley and then up over the hills.

It's easy to gaze at this landscape and appreciate its many colors, its complex and layered history, and to lose yourself in musings of all the years that have passed here, all the mystery of ancient lives that unfolded here. In fact, it's not at all difficult to imagine the woolly mammoth still plodding along these hills, or a Roman sentry standing watch over a vital pass. Looking up at the night sky, you can see the moon and the far away stars that reflect the mystery of our own experience, and in such a moment one can sense a very real connection to something that started so long ago and seemingly will go on forever.

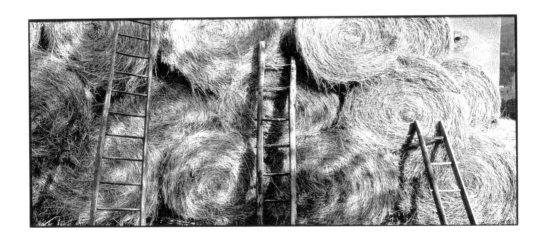

"Ogni giovedì andiamo
a Sestola per il mercato,
la domenica andiamo

"EVERY THURSDAY WE GO TO SESTOLA TO

a messa alle undici;

THE OPEN MARKET, ON SUNDAY WE GO TO MASS AT

quando è bello andiamo

11 O'CLOCK; WHEN THE WEATHER IS NICE

a fare delle belle

WE TAKE NICE WALKS IN THE WOODS. IF IT IS

passeggiate nei

THE RIGHT SEASON WE PICK

boschi e, se è stagione,

MUSHROOMS: PORCINI, GALLETTI, RUSSOLE,

raccogliamo funghi:

"EVERY THURSDAY WE GO TO SESTOLA TO THE OPEN MARKET, ON SUNDAY WE GO TO MASS AT 11 O'CLOCK; WHEN THE WEATHER IS NICE WE TAKE NICE WALKS IN THE WOODS. IF IT IS THE RIGHT SEASON WE PICK MUSHROOMS: PORCINI, GALLETTI, RUSSOLE, OVULI, DENTINI, CHIODINI..."

porcini, galletti,
russole, ovuli, dentini,
chiodini..."

NE SA PIÙ UN
MATTO A
AN INSANE KNOWS MORE IN HIS OWN HOUSE
CASA PROPRIA
THAN A SANE AT SOMEONE ELSE'S HOUSE
CHE UN
SAVIO A CASA
D'ALTRI

P

LA GENTE

Maybe it's because the land itself is relatively young and geologically active, but the people who live in and around Vesale are considered extremely lively and restless, willful, and handsome. Yet in their eyes one discerns a wizened sense of calm, as if they understand precisely who they are and why they are here. Lusty and strong, the people of Vesale are also sincere, intelligent, candid to a fault. A girl who grew up not far from here told me her people have a special kind of courage that enables them to enjoy life in ways that are simple, sober and uncluttered. That very point is evident in the manner in which they express themselves. The voices in Vesale are calm and their language is direct and unpretentious.

Ermelina Querciagrossa, who is now 77 years old, embodies all these virtues. Although getting on in years, she manages to bake seven or eight loaves of rustic mountain bread each week. She bakes in a wood-burning oven, and takes full advantage of the assistance offered by her two sons and their wives. One might precisely and painstakingly follow Ermelina's recipe for bread, but the texture and taste of her bread cannot be replicated. That's because her bread is flavored with this land, this water, the burning wood and the breeze that fans this fire. It's all in the bread, which Ermelina shapes by hand the same way her grandmother and great grandmother did before her.

Whether baking bread, making wine, or preparing the table for lunch, there is a practiced routine for all things. And the family knows every step by heart, as if it were a dance. Davide brings in the wood. Ermelina kneads the dough. No directions are necessary, no criticisms called for. They work with grace and serenity, confident that the results will be just right.

And it's astonishing to realize just how hard these people work. In fact, they are always busy—polishing floors, potting flowers, knitting scarves and sweaters. In Vesale, people believe that God gives you 80 years of life, and that you must fill them up with pleasurable labor. So they work within themselves, never revealing the stress of physical effort. For them work is just another part of life, whether carrying a wheel of cheese to the truck or lugging milk pails through the barn, the task is accomplished comfortably and with grace.

"Perché non ho mai voluto andare via da Vesale? Non saprei. Tutto era qui. Ci sto bene. Non ci manca niente. La gente è buona..."

The Family

LA FAMIGLIA

Here, as it is throughout Italy, the family remains the centerpost of social experience, and deeply intertwined with family are matters of food, religion and celebration. Vesale is a town with one church, one store and one restaurant. It's impossible for the citizens there to imagine the need for another church, or store, or restaurant. That might disrupt the unity of this small community, add the pretense of sophistication, maybe even sow seeds of division and jealousy. Why have more, when one is enough? And in that regard, the various families of Vesale form a single family that upholds tradition and honors a common heritage.

At no time is this sense of unity more evident than during the festival of La Madonna della Santa Provvidenza, which takes place on the first Sunday of every August. It is a religious event, a homecoming and three-day family reunion rolled into one. There is music and dancing, a carnival with games and a parade, and, of course, there is feasting. All the local favorites are prepared and generously served in honor of the Madonna and the spirit of family. Local wine and cold cuts of prosciutto and salami are offered along with crescentine and the region's famous cheese, Parmigiano Reggiano.

Outside the men play ruzzolone which involves rolling a specially made wheel of cheese past obstacles to a distant target. Sometimes the wheel is made of wood, but in either case the object of ruzzolone is the same. Like horseshoes or boccie ball the winner is the one who lands closest to the goal. This is a serious game, observed with as much passion as it is played. People crowd around to cheer their favorite players because skill and honor are at stake. And of course the loser must buy dinner.

In Vesale, during the festival, the games and rituals generate new memories to layer upon those that came before. In celebration, as in daily routine, they honor the traditions of family and of faith. As the accordions breathe out the gypsy rhythms and rustic harmonies, Ermelina and her friends watch the youngsters dance the liscio just as they did so many years ago. These are songs and dances that hold people together and connect one generation to the next. There is meaning and ritual in everything, and while the expressions are easy and casual, the significance is never lost or misunderstood.

Finché i mali
UNTIL THE PAINS
stanno STAY fuori
OUTSIDE THE
HOUSE, di casa,
THEY HAVE hanno
ANOTHER FACE
un'altra faccia.

The Food

IL CIBO

Growing up in such an environment, one learns to appreciate the essence of fresh vegetables, tree-ripened fruit and herbs straight from the garden. One visiting Ermelina for breakfast can never forget the taste of homemade bread with homemade jam, or the richness of fresh whole milk. The way food is honored and prepared in Vesale is another indication of how the people here stay connected to their past.

The rich and lusty yellow of polenta set against simmering red tomatoes and golden roasted chicken conjures up images, aromas and memories of family, hearth and home. The unusual simplicity of these dishes is masked by complex and intensely personal rituals of preparation. It's the way a grandmother teaches her granddaughter how to roll tortellini in her fingers.

Bread, crescentine, gnocchi fritti, borlenghi, tortellini, rosette, and also zuccherini. They all begin the same, says Ermelina. "You take the wheat flour on a table and shape it like a mountain. Then you make a well." Away from that table, on the wood burning stove, water is boiling, and the room is full of the soft flavor of onions sautéing in oil or butter. There are special, complicated meals for Sunday and other important occasions, but mostly the cooking is simple, not fancy. Soup is the common element of dinner, and the vegetables for soup come directly from the garden—beans, potatoes, carrots, radicchio in winter, and squash in summer.

Ermelina sets the table while the soup simmers, and the conversation turns to reminiscence. "How was the wartime for you?" someone asks.

"It was hard, of course. There was less to eat. Not like now. But we had all we needed. We had the vegetable garden, and we always had flour to make crescentine and bread, corn flour to make polenta and we had chestnuts to make castagnaccio. We had milk from the cows to make ricotta and butter. We had hens and therefore eggs for frittata. We had everything, really."

We still do.

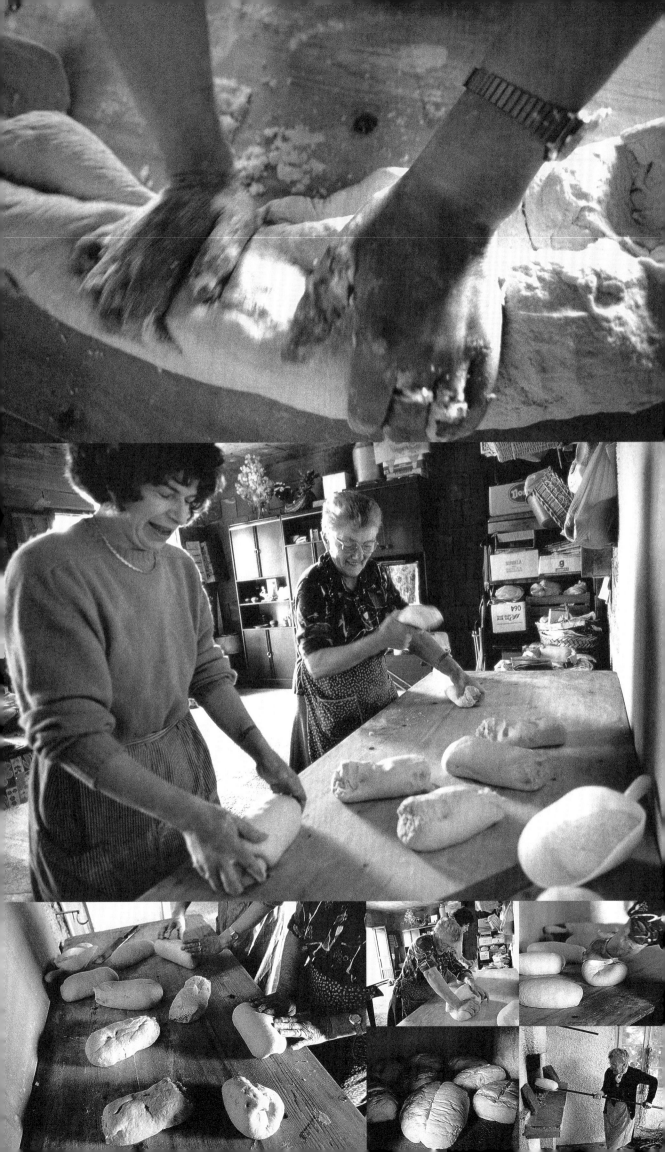

POLLO
IN UMIDO

This kind of chicken is usually served with polenta but also with crescentine.

You need a whole chicken cut into pieces, a small onion cut very thin, a glass of white wine, two glasses of tomato puree, a little bit of oil, fresh herbs and salt. 1. In a nice pot cook the onion and then brown the chicken in a little bit of oil. Add salt and fresh herbs like rosemary or sage or what you have. 2. When it is nice and brown add the white wine and after a while the tomato puree. You may also need a little water if it is too thick. 3. Then let it cook slowly. If it cooks slowly the results are better. Check it occasionally and add water if it dries out too much. If the chicken is young it will cook faster, if it is old it will take a little more, but should be done in about an hour.

POLENTA *To make polenta you need nice yellow corn flour.*
1. Put a big pot of fresh water on the stove and bring it to a boil, add some salt. 2. Then drop in the yellow flour but do it slowly, mixing it fast with a wooden spoon. Keep an eye on it and mix it frequently so that it doesn't become lumpy. Allow it to cook for about half an hour. 3. When it is ready turn it on a serving dish. Eat it with ragù or tomato sauce, with sausages, other meat or simply with butter and parmigiano cheese.

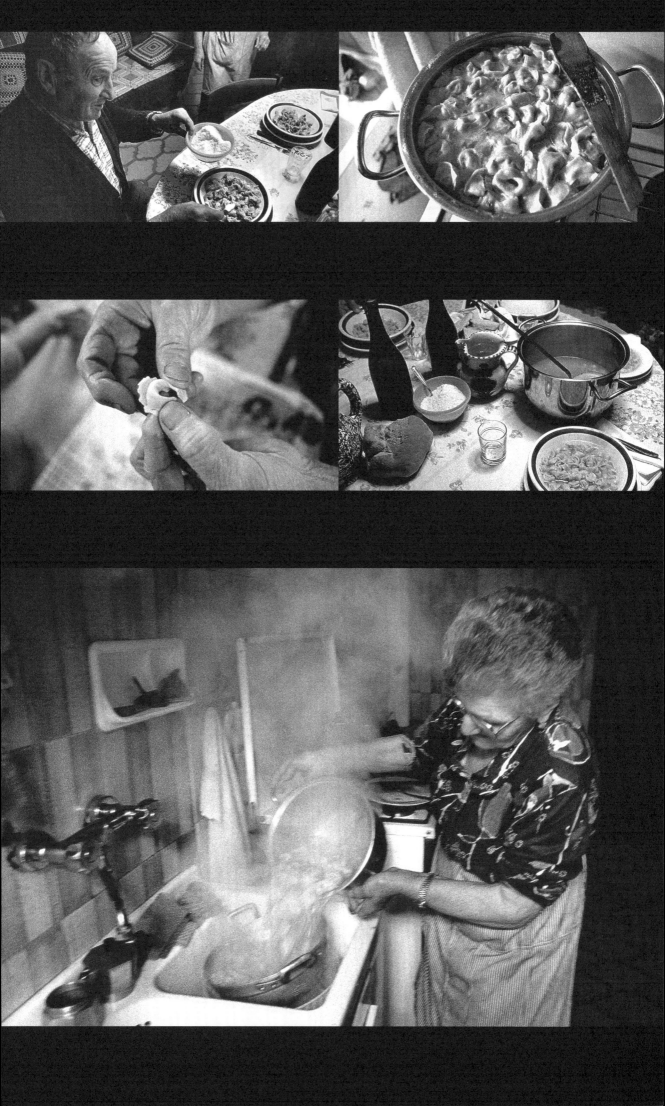

"A me

la polenta

piace

un po' più

tenera, a mio

marito

un po' più

"I LIKE MY POLENTA TO BE SOFT, MY HUSBAND LIKES IT DENSE, SO I MAKE IT NEITHER SOFT NOR DENSE AND WE ARE ALL HAPPY."

solida,

allora

la faccio

non tenera

e non

solida, che

siam

contenti

tutti."

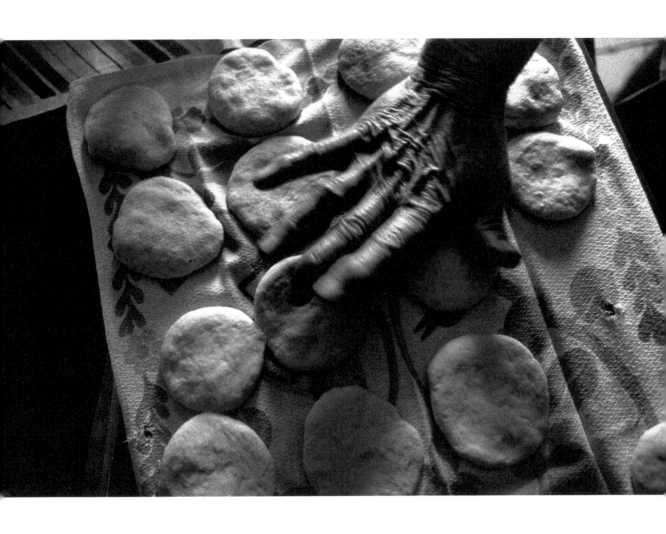

CRESCENTINE

For six to eight people

1. Put one kilo of flour as a mountain on the working surface and make a well. 2. Dissolve 50 grams of yeast in a little bit of warm water and put the yeast in the well. Add water, about half a liter, and a pinch of salt. If you like put a drop of olive oil, but it is not necessary. 3. Make a nice dough. 4. It should not be too hard or too soft but right to the touch. 5. Leave it on the working surface, or another warm place with no draft, covered with a pot. Leave it for a good two hours. 6. When it is risen, punch down and work the dough very shortly, then divide it into small balls, each one as big as an egg. 7. Take each ball and flatten it with your hands or the rolling pin. They should be about half a centimeter thick. 8. To cook them you need special forms, tigelle made with terracotta, or now they sell metal ones. You warm them up on top of the stove. So, you layer the dough and the forms. The crescentine cook this way, but you have to pay attention not to let them burn, and turn them often. 9. When they are done you eat them with what you like: prosciutto, lard, other cold cuts, parmigiano, other cheese, garlic, rosemary...

TORTA DI TAGLIATELLINE

*this recipe requires freshly prepared tagliatelline,
the crust made of pasta frolla and a cream.*

1. Put the flour as a mountain on the working surface and make a well.
2. Add 2 to 3 eggs and work the dough. Let the dough stand for a few minutes and then put it through the pasta machine and cut it as tagliatelline.
3. For the pasta frolla you need 200 grams of flour, 200 grams of sugar, 100 grams of butter, a measure of baking powder and two eggs. Mix all and put the dough in a pie plate. 4. Then you need 200 grams of amaretti cookies, crushed, 250 grams of blanched almonds, crushed, 200 grams sugar, a small glass of almond liqueur, a little bit of grated nutmeg and three eggs. You mix it all together in a nice cream. 5. Then you layer the cream on top of the pasta frolla and then you put the tagliatelline and then the cream again and then you finish with tagliatelline. 6. Top the fresh pasta with small pieces of butter and put it in the preheated oven at medium temperature for 45-50 minutes or until it comes out golden brown.

A SBAGLIARE

IF YOU MAKE A MISTAKE BECAUSE OF HASTE

IN FRETTA

YOU'LL THEN HAVE TO CRY SLOWLY.

SI PIANGE ADAGIO

ERBAZZONE

Have ready a crust made with pasta frolla.

1. For the pasta frolla you need 200 grams of flour, 200 grams of sugar, 100 grams of butter, a measure of baking powder and two eggs. 2. Mix all together and put the dough in a pie plate. 3. Then you have to blanch 300 grams of spinach and mash them well. Also toast and mash 100 grams of blanched almonds. 4. When they are at room temperature you add these to 350 grams of ricotta, 300 grams of sugar, a small glass of sassolino or other anise liqueur and 3 whipped egg whites. Work all this together but not too much. The green of the spinach and the white of the ricotta should still make a nice contrast. 5. Pour the cream over the pasta frolla in the pie plate. You may arrange strips of pasta frolla on the top. 6. Bake in the preheated oven at medium temperature for about 45 minutes. It is done when a toothpick inserted in the middle comes out clean.

Casa mia, casa mia,

HOME, HOME, EVEN IF YOU ARE VERY SMALL,

per piccina che tu sia, tu mi

YOU LOOK TO ME BIG AS AN ABBEY.

sembri una badia.

Bella, or beautiful, has always been the underlying intention for creating this book. When Paul Elledge first shared with me his photographs of Vesale, Italy, more than three years ago, I was immediately struck by the spirit, elegance, and simplicity of the images. Together we felt we could create something honest and wonderful for a larger audience. On behalf of all the participants in this project, I am grateful that Mohawk Paper felt equally moved by Paul's images and so readily embraced the creation of this piece. The sophistication and craftsmanship of Mohawk Superfine complements the grace and texture of these images as well as the lives portrayed upon these pages.

JAMES KOVAL

We would like to thank the following people for their
participation and support of this project:

The Querciagrossa family, Aeta Kay, Judy Querciagrossa, Lucia Elledge,
Margo, Jenna, Matthew and Kalee Koval, Steve Ryan, Lisa Kirk,
Mike Noble, Alba Rossa Dwass, Andy Blankenburg, Leasha Overturf, Suzanne Burns,
Meg Pucino, Steve Behen, Marc Hauser, Anna Debecki, Thomas Masters,
Andrew Brown, Giorgio Manjo, Carlo Tartarelli, Studio staff: past and present

These photographs are available in limited editions through Paul Elledge Photography, Inc. 1808 West Grand Avenue, Chicago, Illinois 60622

SPECIFICATIONS

PAPER

Mohawk Superfine is the industry's benchmark for elegant, uncoated papers. Its
surface is resilient, receptive, velvety and spotlessly clean. Mohawk Superfine's archival
quality is renowned internationally: Mohawk Superfine is acid free and exceeds
the standards for purity and pH recommended by the American Library Association.

Jacket: Mohawk Superfine, Softwhite Eggshell, 80 lb. text.
Cover: Mohawk Superfine, Softwhite Eggshell, 100 lb. cover.
Pages 1-10, 91-100: Mohawk Superfine, Softwhite Eggshell, 80 lb. text.
Pages 11-36, 47-56: Mohawk Superfine, White Eggshell, 80 lb. text.
Pages 35-46, 57-90: Mohawk Superfine, Ultrawhite Eggshell, 80 lb. text.

SCANNING FILM AND PRINTING

The original black and white photographs by Paul Elledge were reproduced on a
Linotype-Hell ChromaGraph S3500 and 608 DS scanner as 200-line screen duotones
and 200-line screen tritones using tonal curves designed to reproduce images for
Mohawk Superfine. The 200-line screen film was output on a Linotype-Hell
Herkules Pro Imagesetter and printed on a four-color 40" Heidelberg Speedmaster
at 6500 impressions per hour. The specially mixed inks were manufactured
by Wikoff Color Corporation.

Ink sequence: dense black, match grey, match yellow, and match orange. An off-line
matte spot varnish was added for protection on all heavy solids and images. All black
solids are supported with a 50% screen of match grey.

BINDING

This publication is bound by the "lay-flat" Otabind™ process. The ability to open
this book at any place, and it will remain open, is due to advanced adhesive binding
technology and a patented free-floating cover, of this type of binding.

PROGRAMS

QuarkXPress®, Adobe Photoshop®

FONTS

Adobe Caslon, Adobe Clarendon, Bitstream Commercial Script,
Agfa ATSackers Italian Script, Emigre Filosofia, Emigre Missionary, Font Studio
Ornaments, Emigre Whirligig, Adobe Woodtype Ornaments